Quiet Teacher: How
Introvert Teacher in an

MW01288858

By Bo Miller
https://ispeakpeople.com/

Quiet Teacher: How to Thrive as an Introvert Teacher in an Extroverted World. Copyright © 2017 by Bo Miller

Disclaimer and FTC Notice

I sometimes use affiliate links in the content. This means if you decide to make a purchase, I will get a sales commission. But that doesn't mean my opinion is for sale. Every affiliate link on is to products that I've personally used and found useful. Please do your own research before making any purchase online.

Your Free Gift

As a way of saying *thank you* for checking out this book, I'm giving you the FREE audiobook companion.

You can download it by CLICKING HERE.

(If the link above doesn't work, copy and paste this one into your browser: **https://ispeakpeople.com/quiet-teacher/**)

Dedication

This book is dedicated to…

My wife Kandra, for her faithful support and encouragement as I continue to learn about myself and try new things

My parents, for helping me learn to read and write

My teachers, Leslie Spurrier and Deann Buffington for inspiring me and encouraging me to write

My mentor, Jay Weaver, for getting me started

Table of Contents

Introduction

The Lack of Resources

At the time of this writing, books for introverts on how to teach in a way that works for them are scarce. After spending some time perusing Amazon.com, I only found a small number of texts, and the suggested works addressed few of the problems I've encountered because of my introversion over my teaching career. I imagine you've found few books that address the problems you face as an introverted teacher and that help you maximize your unique gifts.

A Rough Go of It

By the end of this school year, I will have completed eight years as an elementary school teacher. Mine has been a difficult road with many ups and downs. I can't remember a single struggle-free year where lack of energy and motivation weren't a problem. Some years, because of colleagues, students, or other circumstances, I faced these obstacles on a daily basis.

That said, I'm incredibly blessed: I have the privilege of teaching in what's widely regarded as one of the best elementary schools in my region. The faculty are welcoming and supportive, and the school environment is generally uplifting.

Furthermore, as a male teacher in an elementary setting, I have the privilege of working with at least ten other men. This is far from typical. Usually, male elementary teachers are few and far between, so it's rare to have so many men teaching together in the same building.

On top of that, I come from a family of teachers that knows and appreciates the profession. My mom and dad were both teachers, and my sister currently teaches. What's more, my extended family respects and highly regards the teaching profession. This is especially true of my wife who, though she hasn't been through a teaching program, is a teacher at heart.

So having enjoyed such incredible circumstances, I had to ask: *What's the problem?*

After several rough years of experience and a lot of time learning about myself, others, and what makes them and me tick, I think I've arrived at the source: it has to do with the fact that **I'm an introvert teaching in an extroverted world**. For too long, I've compared myself with other teachers and seen a significant difference between my style and energy and theirs. When I compare myself to the way they teach, I feel inadequate and out-of-place.

I've tried to teach the way they do, but my efforts always fall short. I *can* squeeze in a couple high-energy days fueled by coffee, will-power, and sheer determination, but by the middle of the week, I'm always dragging. And, definitely, by the end of the week, I'm ready to crawl into bed for the weekend. I want nothing to do with people.

The Aim of This Book

Admittedly, a lot of the suffering I endured was my fault. I was ignorant.

Early on, I tried to stay late at school too many nights. I tried to coach volleyball, complete graduate school classes, maintain a social life, and come in on the weekends. Exhaustion was the norm for me.

In the last few years, however, I've learned - and am still learning - how to lean into to my introverted strengths and teach in a way that works for me. While I still confront many of the same problems, I'm doing far better than I ever had before.

In this book I want to share what's been working for me in order to help you enjoy teaching more. I want to help you discern your own unique gifts and suggest some practical approaches and strategies that will hopefully help you inject more joy into the job you have liked on so many different occasions.

If you've ever wrestled with a lack of energy, compared yourself with others, or wondered how to teach in a way that honors your introverted personality, I wrote this book for you. I hope it gives you courage to soldier on for your good, the good of your family, the welfare of the students you've touched, your coworkers, and the good of your school in general. Your students and coworkers need you and your unique gifts.

This book will first address the problems facing introverted teachers. It will then offer solutions to those problems by...

- Showing you how to establish boundaries in and outside of your

classroom and in your teacher-student and collegial relationships;
- Helping you discover what energizes you and excites you most;
- Helping you tame your schedule;
- Showing you how to re-energize;
- Showing you how to guard your mental energy, stay organized, and improve your efficiency.

The Scope

This book is not a comprehensive treatment of the problems facing introvert teachers. Instead, I intend it to be the start of a conversation of how introvert teachers can modify their schedules, environments, teaching styles, and approaches to better suit their unique personalities. I hope that this book helps you better understand yourself and others around you. And I hope it also helps you enjoy your job more. May it lead to still more resources and conversations for introvert teachers.

Furthermore, I recognize my perspective is limited. Though I endeavor to, perhaps, one day teach at the college level, my experience is limited to the elementary classroom. I hope, however, that this won't dissuade you from reading on. If you are a middle school or high school teacher, a college professor, or if you teach in any other setting, I believe this book will have helpful advice and insights to offer you. Regardless of where you teach or what you teach, all forms of teaching are similar to some extent. So read and take from this work what's helpful for you, and disregard whatever isn't.

How It's Meant to Be Used

Please use this book in whatever manner suits you. Read it word-for-word from cover to cover, or pick the chapters that deal with the things that are giving you the most trouble at any given time. I intend this to be a handbook of sorts. Its order should lend itself to topical research. So feel free to scan the table of contents for particular problems you're dealing with.

PART ONE

Part I: Fish Out of Water: The Face of Introvert Teachers

CHAPTER ONE

How to Tell If You're an Introvert

Before we go any further in this book, we need to have the same definition for *introvert*. In addition, if you've picked up this book, chances are good that you know you're an introvert. But maybe you don't. The goal of this chapter, then, will be to find a common definition for introvert and to help you determine whether or not you are one.

Contrary to popular belief, the word introvert neither means recluse nor does it mean antisocial. Introverts don't dislike people. The word introvert, rather, deals more with where a person focuses his energy and how he recharges.

Psychologist Carl Jung first used the term *introvert* to describe a personality preference in the early 1900s. It became part of his personality classification system which is today the Myers-Briggs personality system. Jung said that all people are either *introverted* or *extroverted*. The extroverts among us get energy from engaging with a variety of people and in a variety of experiences. They talk to think and need activity to stimulate their brains. Introverts, however, prefer to have a few deep relationships, think to talk, and recharge alone.

Mutually Exclusive?
Aren't the words introvert and teacher mutually exclusive? A teacher is surrounded by people all day long. She'd go nuts if she were an introvert, right?

I hear that kind of talk a lot. But it's misguided. Many introverts choose teaching for a career. The term introvert does not denote a lack of social skills or an aversion to people. Many introverts enjoy being around people and find purpose and meaning in helping them. So don't assume you're not an introvert just because you decided to become a teacher.

What Interests You?
Are you the type of person who's friends with everybody and considers many people friends? Or do you have a handful of deep, close relationships? Although an introvert may know a lot of people, he'll likely only consider a handful of them to be true friends. As you ponder this point, bear in mind that you may not fall squarely into one camp or the other, and that's okay. Think instead, *Which option describes me more accurately?*

Also, consider what you know. Do you know a little about a lot of things and prefer to talk about a wide variety of subjects? Or do you major on a few specific interests? Introverts prefer to go deep on a few topics that really capture their interest.

How Do You Process?
Admittedly, we all process aloud from time to time. But where do you do your best thinking? Do you need to talk out your ideas to see where you land and what you understand? Do you like to bounce most of your ideas off of other people? Or do you need time alone to think, make decisions, and draw your own conclusions? Introverts are usually internal processors who spend the majority of their time in the world of thoughts and ideas.

How Do You Recharge?
After a long, hard week of teaching, what would excite you more? An action-packed weekend out on the town, enjoying concerts, eating out, visiting with friends, and staying up late? Or a quiet, relaxing time at home with a book, a movie, your favorite music, and maybe a friend or two. Most introverts would choose the latter - at least most of the time.

How Do You Communicate?
When you express yourself, what's your preferred mode of communication? Speaking or writing? Most introverts far prefer writing to speaking. That's not to say introverts are poor speakers. Some are very good. It's just that writing is better suited to the introverted way of life. It allows for reflection, analysis, and careful synthesis of ideas. And it's usually a primarily independent activity.

Extroverts, on the other hand, prefer the social spark that conversation brings. They need the back-and-forth. Talking actually helps them process their ideas.

Brain Wiring
In The Introvert Advantage, Marty Olsen Lani, Psy. D. explains that introvert and extrovert brains are actually wired differently. Extroverts have a shorter pathway of thought and are less sensitive to certain neurotransmitters. Introverts, on the other hand, have longer thought pathways and are very sensitive to neurotransmitters. As a result, extroverts need larger doses of activity to be alert and at their best. But this isn't the case for introverts. The same amount of stimulation an extrovert needs would probably be overkill for an introvert.

Consider a party, for instance. An extrovert can really get fired up by all the conversation, loud music, and activity that come with a party atmosphere. But the same environment would produce the opposite effect in an introvert, who'd far prefer a deep conversation with a friend in a quiet hole-in-the-wall cafe. When you do find introverts at parties, you'll find them on the outskirts of the crowd and in the side rooms, away from the hustle and bustle.

The Majority Rule
As you think about where you fall on the spectrum when it comes to the

introvert and extrovert camps, it's helpful to realize we all demonstrate introverted *and* extroverted behaviors from time to time. No one ever acts just as an introvert or an extrovert. To determine, then, whether you're an introvert or extrovert, figure out which camp you're in most of the time. In *Self-Promotion for Introverts*, Nancy Ancowitz wisely suggests you ponder whether introvert or extrovert traits describe you best "more than 50% of the time."

Assuming you confirmed or discovered you're an introvert - or maybe you're just a curious extrovert - it's time to take a look at what draws most introverts to teaching. And that's the subject of the next chapter.

CHAPTER TWO

Why We Teach

What draws introverts to the teaching profession? What makes it such a meaningful career or personality fit that typically quiet-loving people regularly and purposefully go into teaching in the first place? Four key reasons come to mind.

We *Do* Like People

As I mentioned before, many introverts do like being around people. Introverts and time with people are not mutually exclusive. The main difference between people-loving introverts and extroverts is that introverts will eventually run out of energy and need to get away by themselves. While social interaction charges extroverts up, it drains introverts.

More specifically, many introverts love to help other people and see teaching as a great way to do just that. What better way is there to help someone, after all, than to give her the skills she needs to succeed in life? And when you're in a classroom with students day in and day out, you have a unique opportunity to speak into their lives that you'll find nowhere else. Furthermore, teaching allows introverts to establish student-teacher relationships built on trust and gives them a platform from which they can encourage and inspire young minds.

And let's not overlook the "Aha!" moment. Ask any teacher, and he'll tell you that his favorite moments are the ones when a student finally gets a concept or learns a skill. It's especially rewarding when the student has struggled for a long time - or other teachers have given up on that student in the past. Then, when the lightbulb turns on, it's true joy.

Personally, one of the most rewarding aspects of teaching is helping students learn to get along with each other. I enjoy teaching children how to listen, ask questions, and demonstrate interest in others. I also enjoy helping kids work out their problems and reconcile. I think this is the case for introvert teachers who are part counselor at heart.

Finally, most introverts are great listeners. This makes them especially well-suited for work with people. Stephen Covey, author of the *7 Habits of Highly Effective People*, taught that we can avoid most interpersonal conflicts by "[seeking] first to understand, then to be understood," and students need to see this in practice. Who's a better fit to model this than introverts? Perhaps just as important, a listening ear is what many students are craving. They appreciate chances to share what excites them and like knowing they have someone with whom they can share their problems. Their introvert teacher might be the one soul in whom they can confide.

We're Born to Be Experts

Another aspect of teaching that attracts introverts is the opportunity to become subject area specialists. Introverts generally know a lot about a few topics. They like to plumb the depths of an interest and know it inside and out. As a result, they're in a sense born to be experts of their preferred interests.

This was one of the main things that drew me to teaching. Even when I was a boy, I got excited about learning a subject thoroughly. In first and second grade, I was reading - or at least pretending to read - books on herpetology and ichthyology, while my classmates were reading picture books. And the opportunity to become a subject area specialist is still one of the parts of the job that I like best. Fun, for me, is a free afternoon with a book - or a late night researching a topic of interest on the internet. It's nice when your job rewards your desire to learn.

We Like the Structure

Still other factors attract introverts to teaching. One of them is the order and structure that's inherent in every school. A lot of introvert teachers - though not all - like the structure and routine that come with school. They like to know what to expect. Every year, without fail, the calendar will progress the same way. The school day will be the same length, and the periods and bell schedules will stay consistent.

Even the buildings will be organized, and each teacher will maintain order within his room. Teachers are responsible for teaching and enforcing school rules and expectations. So they teach procedures that detail how to do assignments, how to walk in the hallway, and what to do in the case of an emergency. These layers of strict norms and expectations, which everybody knows, comfort many introvert teachers.

In some regards, teaching also affords an introvert privacy that he can depend on. He can create, in a sense, his own little world, within his classroom. As long as aides, supervisors, or other teachers aren't slipping in all the time, he's pretty much got the place to himself. Once he's taught students his expectations, he's set for the rest of year.

We Want to Change the World

Other introvert teachers just want to change the world. They feel called to a greater mission and have a strong sense of purpose. They want to leave the world better than they found it and teach others how to be generous. They want to break the cycles, bridge the gaps, and change lives. And they know that teaching is one of the best ways to do it all quietly and intentionally.

Those are a few reasons why introverts love the teaching profession, but it's by no means an exhaustive list. In the next chapter, we'll explore what makes teaching as an introvert so challenging.

CHAPTER THREE

What Drains Us

If teaching is such a great fit, then why do introverts tire of it? What's so draining? This chapter will attempt to answer those questions in light of what the last chapter revealed about introvert nature.

A Lack of Alone Time

To thrive, introverts need downtime. They need privacy and quiet to charge their batteries, but during the school day, opportunities to recharge are few and far between. While there is a prep period, it's seldom long enough, and someone or something usually interrupts it, for instance, needing to call a parent or addressing a behavior concern. Other times, it's a meeting. Teachers plan collaboratively more and more, and that means working with another person. And then there are meetings, regular data meetings to review student progress and meetings with parents, supervisors, counselors, psychologists, and home-to-school visitors.

Perhaps lunch offers a glimmer of hope. That's an opportunity for quiet, right? Unfortunately, many introvert teachers feel compelled to eat with their colleagues. They don't want to appear cold, aloof, or standoffish, no matter how much they'd really like a half hour to themselves. So their much-needed alone time yet again slips away.

A Constant Struggle for Quiet

Each day of teaching is a battle for quiet. As soon as students enter the room, the noise begins. When class begins, the problem doesn't go away. The introvert teacher has to keep in mind that he's got extroverts in his classroom too. These students *need* to talk in order to process, so he's got to build meaningful conversation into his lesson. Staying calm and focused, teaching in a way students can learn, and doing it all while the phone or intercom are bound to interrupt you once or twice a day is no easy job.

When you're "on" all day, it's easy to run out of steam. I'm sure you know the feeling, when you're the center of attention, and everybody's got a question that's got to be answered RIGHT NOW. As an elementary school teacher, these are the times that drain me most. When kids barrage me with nonstop questions, forgetting to raise their hands, I can feel my batteries actively draining. I just want to crawl under my desk or run away, but I'm stuck in the middle needing to figure a way to deal with it.

Conflict
Dealing with people all day also spells conflict. Kids think differently, and they don't all like each other, so it's no surprise that teachers are called on to resolve the conflict. It doesn't have to be a fistfight either. It can just be two kids shouting at each other, or it may even be one child who wants to argue with everything you say. The argumentative child is a real energy drain for me. If you've got more than one of those special cherubs in your classroom, bless you.

Environmental Noise
Even if a teacher has his classroom environment under control and has a relatively quiet classroom, he's got to fight other noise. Every time students transition from one class to another, they want to talk. In the hallway, they talk when they're not supposed to. In the cafeteria and on the playground, they scream and talk. No matter how many times you address the issue, the problem eventually resurfaces.

If you've ever had the unfortunate responsibility of supervising the cafeteria or another loud room, you've no doubt found it to be particularly draining. Sensing freedom, kids talk loudly, freely, and incessantly. And as time passes, the volume rises. In no time, neighbors are shouting over neighbors so that their conversational partner across the table can hear what they have to say. Meanwhile, the introvert teacher's battery is rapidly losing its charge.

Even the physical setup of the school affects an introvert's energy. The fluorescent lights, the white walls and bright colors, and the shiny surfaces in the hallway can be overstimulating when you have to deal with them all day long. Your extroverted neighbor is blaring music from her classroom, trying to get her blood pumping for the morning. What she doesn't know is that what's getting her fired up is working on your nerves.

Post-People Responsibility
When the kids finally go home, the job isn't over. There are papers to grade, documents to file, emails to send, and lessons to write. It's easy to spend a couple extra hours (at least!) at work every day to feel like you're on top of your game. And if you are an elementary school teacher, you've got a whole variety of lesson materials to prepare. Figuring out what to do first and how to prioritize can get frustrating. If you're not staying late after school, you're probably taking paperwork home - at least some of the time. So you spend your precious downtime working on schoolwork when you'd prefer to be relaxing with a book, listening to music, or doing something quietly.

Extracurricular Activities
Add to that the fact that many teachers are involved in extracurricular activities as coaches or club advisors. They are the ones in charge of the Girls on

the Run club, the middle school basketball team, or even the varsity tennis squad. While the competition, change of pace, and different environment are in some ways rewarding, the added responsibility still takes a toll.

With all the busyness and noise, the week gets crazy fast and bleeds over into nights and weekends. Consequently, crucial rest and quiet activities that revive the spirit get put off, and the introvert teacher ends up feeling exhausted and burned out. All of the sudden, the job that she loved so much at first begins to lose its sparkle.

Is there any way for her to redeem the job that she really does enjoy deep down inside? Absolutely! Let's start with boundaries, the subject of the next chapter.

PART TWO

Part II: Setting Up Boundaries

CHAPTER FOUR

Defining Boundaries

One of the best ways introvert teachers can adapt their teaching jobs so that they better complement their personalities is to set up boundaries. Boundaries are both physical and interpersonal. In this chapter will take a look at several ways you can use boundaries to show students, other teachers, administrators, and the people you interact with each day at work where the line is in order to preserve your energy.

Physical Boundaries

To quickly obtain more privacy and quiet, an introvert teacher can start by organizing his room in a way that allows fewer distractions and turns it into a quiet sanctuary.

I experimented with this idea for the first time this year when I moved my desk from the front of the room, away from the door, to the back of the room. While this makes teaching slightly more challenging, considering my interactive whiteboard is at the front of the room and my computer, to which it's connected, is at the back, most of the time it's no big deal. Along with the added benefit of having more room at the front of the classroom with my desk out of the way, I've experienced far fewer interruptions during planning hours. In the past, coworkers would walk by my room, poke their heads in, and stop to talk. But now, as they're walking down the hallway, they are less tempted to pop into my room. All they see is an empty classroom, and they don't know whether or not I'm at my desk. Consequently, they stop in less. Thanks to this setup, I have way more focus time where I can crank out work in quiet.

My desk doesn't just cut down on interruptions with coworkers, though. It helps obtain extra quiet time at the end of the day too. After my class is done with their last scheduled, formal educational activity, I ask them to grab their belongings and pull out homework or a book. Recently, I've been retreating to my desk during this time to get some extra work done. It's a definite plus having the extra work time. I almost never had quiet at the end of the day in the past. Now, however, I'm able to keep an eye on everyone while I churn out some of the tasks on my to-do list.

Another part of my setup this year that's helped quite a bit is a lamp that I added to my desk. It was an easy, pain-free addition that made a big difference.

Whenever I'm working by myself, I turn off the fluorescent lights - that drive my eyes and brain crazy - and I work in the relative peacefulness of a lights-out classroom. The only exception is the desk lamp I have turned on. The soft glow is better on my eyes and more than enough to see by.

Because I have my desk in the back of the room, people assume that I'm not in when the lights are out at the front. More than once the janitor has come in, surprised to find me working. He didn't even know I was there!

Another consideration when you're setting up your room is the colors you have on the wall. I'm not really one to talk about classroom design - or any design for that matter, but I do know that bright, intense colors can be overstimulating. If color schemes throughout the rest of your school are a bit too intense, consider decorating your classroom with soft, calm colors.

Nonverbal Boundaries

Along with the physical setup of your room, you can gain more quiet and minimize interruptions through intentional nonverbal communication.

One of the strategies that I'm using this year is the "move with purpose technique." I learned this strategy from Tim Ferriss's book The 4-Hour Work Week. Whenever I need to get stuff done - or I'm not in the mood to talk to other people - I walk quickly and determinedly to my intended destination. I make sure my gate and facial expressions convey that I'm a man on a mission. I don't frown, grit my teeth, or anything like that - I just walk extra quickly. Other teachers are naturals when it comes to reading nonverbal language. They know to leave me alone because I've got to get stuff done.

And on the flip side, beware of moving casually and too much casual conversation. If you make either a habit, you'll teach other people that you're always available and free to talk to. You DON'T want them to internalize this. It's a great way to throw away a lot of your time. But in the end, it is a balance. You want to have good relationships with coworkers without sending the wrong signals.

Time Boundaries

If you've been at your school more than a few months, you probably know the rhythms and routines of your coworkers. You know when the copier is free, when coworkers are in the faculty lounge, and when everyone's congregating in the hallway to chew the fat. Use this to your advantage. Plan your work around the schedule, and aim to be at the copier, the faculty lounge, the teacher planning room, the office - wherever - when the majority of folks are away. This will keep you from getting sucked into conversations and help your preserve your energy.

For your own sanity and a better work-life balance, consider placing boundaries on the time you allot to the completion of schoolwork. As I've already admitted, I used to do schoolwork at all hours. I would grade over the weekends, work on projects over the holidays, and plan away from my classroom. In the end, this was a bad idea because I allowed myself to be less productive during school hours, and I justified my actions by assuming that I had the time to spare. It was also bad for my energy: I didn't leave myself adequate time away from school that I needed to recharge. While I did leave my classroom, when I took my work with me, I still didn't have enough of a break. I thought about the work that I needed to do whenever I wasn't doing it. To be the best teacher I could be, I needed to free myself from that worry. I needed time when I wasn't thinking about students or schoolwork.

This year, I've done a much better job of relegating my work to the school building and the time that I am at work. As a result I've been much more productive during work hours and far better rested after weekends and holiday breaks. I typically allot an extra hour before or after work because I know that I will need more time than my prep period affords me. But besides that, with the exception of projects and papers that I need to grade, I don't allow myself any extra time. Over and over again, I amaze myself with how much I get done *when I have to*. So before, my problem must never have been a lack of time, but, rather, poor management of it. Parkinson's Law sums it up well: *Work expands so as to fill the time available for its completion.*

One especially powerful rule I've given myself is that I will grade tests the day I collect them. As soon as students leave, I sit down at my desk and start powering through assessments. Doing this frees my mind up for the evening and the next day. I don't have to carry around the mental baggage that comes when I'm worrying about ungraded tests. And if you don't think that your prep time and the hour you have after school is enough time for you to grade tests in one day, I'll share a great tool with you in the Tech Tools chapter of this book. It really cuts back my work load.

To promote peace and rest, I've even placed "quiet hours" on my school communications. For instance, I don't check email after I leave the school building. (This got a lot easier when I removed my email account from my smartphone!) Also, I set the precedent that I'm not free for phone calls and parent-communication after a certain hour. Not all parents will like this at first, but there's seldom a case when you can't connect with one of them before school, during the day, or just after students leave. They'll learn to respect you for your decision.

The next three chapters in this section of the book will extend our boundaries discussion in this chapter. But the chapters will also provide strategies for dealing with the three major stressors for introvert teachers: phone calls, parent conferences, and meetings. Since you likely deal with phone calls more than the other two, I'll address that issue in the next chapter.

CHAPTER FIVE

Phone Calls

If you're anything like most introverts I know, you probably don't like the phone. Talking on the phone requires quick responses with little time to think. Communication is made doubly hard because there are no nonverbal cues to work with. Phone calls can be a real drain.

For a long time, I did everything I could to avoid the phone. I put off calling parents, made up excuses for not calling coworkers back, sent emails, and went in person instead. While I didn't have to call people as much, I wasn't nearly as efficient as I could have been. It wasn't until my third or fourth year of teaching that I really started to make progress with the phone. I learned some techniques that helped me circumvent problems with parents. I also learned how to decrease the pain I was experiencing when talking. I still don't like talking on the phone, but I've learned a few things that make it more bearable.

Write Out Your Thoughts Ahead of Time

If you have to talk on the phone, do yourself a favor, and write out your thoughts in advance. Doing so will help you relax, and talking will be much easier when you've already planned what you're going to say. If you work closely with another colleague, you may even want to bounce ideas off of him (or her) prior to getting on the phone. Those suggestions and feedback can give you confidence before you ever pick up the handset.

Tag Team It

When I make calls at work, one of my favorite strategies for beating phone anxiety is to place calls along with another coworker. We use the speaker phone and take turns talking. Working as a team takes a lot of pressure off both of us. We have more processing time when we take turns talking. And the person we're talking with enjoys more thorough answers to his questions because he hears from both of us.

Swallow that Frog

Zig Ziglar said, "If you're going to have to swallow a frog, you don't want to have to look at that sucker too long!" That's good advice when it comes to phone conversations. Don't put them off. I used to volunteer to go first for class speeches. Not only did the teacher grade me more leniently, but I avoided the worry that came with anticipating my turn. When you're dreading a phone call, take care of it as soon as possible. You'll save yourself mental and physical energy, get more done the rest of the day, and more than likely find out it wasn't as bad as you thought it'd be.

Batch-Process Calls

This strategy is a lot like Tim Ferriss's email method from the 4-Hour Work Week, only for phone calls. I've adapted his idea for all of us who hate phone calls. Since introverts need quiet to concentrate, one of the challenges of having a phone is managing interruptions. The crazy thing can ring whenever. So you could be deep in thought, making some great progress on a project and instantly get knocked off-course. Why not try turning your phone off? Instead of permitting coworkers and parents to reach you at all hours, let your inbox take calls for you. Then, set up a regular time when you'll get back to them.

You'll have a chance to screen your calls and determine which ones are most important. In addition, you'll be able to guard your think time and multiply your productivity. As a caveat, it would be wise to get permission from your principal or supervisor before giving this method a go. You may also want to let coworkers know what you're doing ahead of time so that they don't get annoyed with you.

Reward Yourself

Let's be frank. You'll probably never love talking on the phone. So how do you motivate yourself? Answer: Plan a reward. Before you talk on the phone, think of what you enjoy doing at work. Maybe it's a conversation with a colleague, a short walk, time reading the newspaper, or a lunch break. Whatever it is, schedule it immediately after the majority of your calls – or your toughest ones. It'll give you something to look forward to and keep you plugging away – even when you don't feel like it.

Stop Over-Analyzing

In general, introverts are predisposed to introspection. We're thinkers. But sometimes it gets us in trouble. An introvert can remember a conversation from years ago, mentally critique it, and perseverate on what went wrong, long after his conversational partner forgot what was said. If you're prone to over-analyzing, cut yourself some slack. Learn from your mistakes, and move on. Over-analyzing will only destroy your confidence while intensifying your phone aversion. Remember the spotlight effect: Most of us imagine the whole world is watching when other people are really tuned into themselves.

Hopefully, you gleaned a strategy or two that'll raise your comfort level or improve your effectiveness on the phone. In the next chapter we'll take a look at how you can set yourself up for greater success during parent-teacher conferences.

CHAPTER SIX

Parent Conferences

My introvert coworkers would do anything to avoid parent conferences, despite the fact that they're usually well-prepared and professional. The pressure of making small talk with people they don't know well - who can at times be hostile - leads them to prefer interacting with children. Hence, the reason they became teachers in the first place.

I share their sentiments. For a long time, I've disliked parent-teacher conferences too. But I'm learning to navigate them more successfully. I'm even starting to enjoy a lot of the parent-teacher conferences I have, even when they're stacked back-to-back. Introvert teachers don't have to suffer through conferences. In this chapter, I'll suggest a number of practical steps you can take to transform your parent-conference experience.

Preparation

You've probably already got this one covered, but just in case... prepare, prepare, prepare. As an introvert, you're great at thinking ahead and researching. Use this strength to your advantage. This year, for all my students, I created a separate note in Evernote (which you can learn more about in the Tech Tools chapter). I added a preview of each student's report card, notes from other teachers, and a behavioral graph. For students who hadn't been following the rules, I dragged digital copies of all their misdemeanors into the file. I also kept a hanging file folder of students' reading work, a district writing assessment, and two journals that the kids wrote on a daily basis, one on different writing prompts and another planning journal that's intended to teach good thinking.

Having all those artifacts within reach relaxed me. I could show the parents what their child had been doing in school and back up what I was saying with examples. Organizing that information and storing it throughout the year gave me a chance to prepare for conferences incrementally so that the final preparation wasn't nearly as cumbersome - or contrived - as it had been in the past.

Seating

I learned from a grad class that one of the most important things you can do is choose your seating wisely. Because your seating location and posture send either a positive or negative message, you should put some thought into the physical set up for your conferences. Many teachers sit across from parents during conferences, but I wouldn't recommend this. Sitting across from parents communicates a hierarchy where they're at the bottom and you're at the top. Parents are already leaving the comfort of their homes to come to school to meet with you. The last thing you want to do is make them more uncomfortable by subconsciously asserting your superiority. Instead, it's better to sit beside parents and look at student progress reports and work together. When you sit across from parents during conferences, you can subtly communicate, when addressing an issue, that they're the problem. But when you sit beside them, you can focus your energies on addressing the issue and not have to feel so concerned that blame is being wrongly accepted. You communicate, "We're a team!"

Mirroring

From time to time, parents get angry during conferences. And teachers aren't always to blame. Unfortunately, Johnny's grades and performance in school just happens to be the straw that breaks the camel's back, and the introvert teacher ends up stuck with an explosive parent. The next time a parent's emotions get the best of her, try mirroring her movements. If she waves her arms, wave your arms in the same fashion and with the same intensity. If she crosses her arms over her chest, do likewise. Similarly, use the same tone and volume she uses when you respond - even if you don't feel the emotions she's feeling. Doing this communicate empathy; the parent will feel listened to and eventually calm down.

I don't know why this works, but it's a great tool to have in your pocket. If a conversation gets heated, it's often not the teacher's fault. But it's nice to know that you've got some tools to calm the situation down.

Missed Conferences

In addition to emotional parents, you'll likely face some no shows. A parent says he's going to come but then never appears. When this happens, you can wave it off and not reschedule, or you can knock that conference off your to-do list right away. I recommend the latter. I use two substitutes for in-person conferences that get the job done well, help me communicate student progress, and keep me on schedule: phone conferences and video overviews.

As I mentioned earlier, I'm not a huge fan of phone calls. Nonetheless, the phone is a super tool for taking care of conferences because it's an effective way to end a discussion with limited awkwardness. If a parent misses a meeting, dial her up, and give her the gist of the details that you were going share during the meeting. Then, check that conference off your list.

I also enjoy sending video overviews to parents. Since I've already taken the time to create an organized file with student information and a progress report for the year - and since it's digital - I like to use video to *show* parents what I'd normally talk them through in person. Giving an overview this way is effective because it keeps the sharing to a minimum - there's no back-and-forth. And I can focus on the most salient points. The downside is that there's no discussion. But I always encourage parents to email me back with questions. My videos usually take only 10 minutes to make. I try to limit the time I spend making them to less time than I'd spend in a conference. To learn more about an inexpensive yet effective tool for recording video conferences, check out Screen-Cast-O-Matic in the Tech Tools chapter.

Listening

The best tool I have in my toolbox for conferences, however, is to focus on listening, and that's true for you too. As much as parents want to hear about their child's progress in school, they want to tell you about their child, get to know you, and ask questions. Whenever my goal is to hammer through a list of points, I often skim or skip what parents want most. This is counterproductive and puts me at a disadvantage for the rest of the year. When, however, I take the time to listen and hear from parents, I open up dialogue and a positive relationship that keeps paying dividends.

Best of all, listening is a natural introvert strength. As you sit and listen, you'll be able to process what's on a parent's mind. This active listening and processing will help you discern what parents need to hear most so that you can share only pertinent information. Like a good doctor, you'll know what "medicine" to prescribe.

The One Thing

Are you familiar with the Pareto Principal? It states that 20% of the work produces 80% of the results. It works in almost all areas of life. 20% of the pea plant in a garden produces 80% of the results. 20% of the workers in a company produce 80% of the profit. 20% of the tasks we do produce 80% of the outcomes we're looking for. It stands to reason, then, that some of what we do and share during conferences is more important than other information we share and things we do. In the end, you can save yourself and the parents you meet with time and hassle by deciding ahead of time what the one most important take away is. Ask yourself, What's the ONE thing I want them to understand or do? If I could only communicate one detail, which one would make the biggest difference for the child - or my classroom? Which one would take the monkey off my back? Figure it out, and focus on that ONE THING during the meeting.

The last chapter in this section will address meetings and how you, as an introvert teacher, can worry less about them and contribute more. Let's get to it!

CHAPTER SEVEN

Meetings

Meeting... The word used to make me sick to my stomach. Just hearing it could ruin a perfectly good day. Meetings meant fast thinking and talking, a chance for me to say something stupid, and likely conflict. Count me out.

For a long while, I made it my goal to say as little as possible during meetings. And I did a poor job listening too. It wasn't that I didn't want to hear what others had to say. It's just that I spent a huge portion of the meeting time cooking up my answers to probable questions. I wanted to be ready when called on and didn't want to be caught off guard. I never liked sounding and feeling like an idiot.

I don't dread meetings quite so much anymore. While I can't say that I enjoy them, I can tolerate them largely because of several principles, practices, and strategies that help me participate as an introvert. I offer them to you.

A License to Cut People Off

My biggest pet peeve when it comes to meetings is that it's hard to fit a word in edgewise. Extroverts spend the time we're gathered together clambering over one another with their words and cutting each other off. In the past, when I had a chance to think about what I wanted to contribute and had my comment ready, sharing was nearly impossible. There was almost never an opening. And I felt awful cutting other people off.

I've since learned that this is just the way extroverts process and relate. And they don't take it personally if you cut them off to share an idea. They're going to do it to you no matter what, so you might as well jump into the fray. The problem with cutting people off and interrupting, though, is it can take a lot of energy out of you. And you may feel awful doing it - as if you're treating people poorly. For these reasons, it's wise to wait until you really have something important to say, something that matters to you. But when you do want to share an idea or make an observation, give yourself permission to interject and interrupt. If possible, wait for an opening. But, if none ever appears, take the reigns - just do it as tactfully as you can.

Also realize that, if you're the kind of person that puts yourself in other people's shoes and generally thinks about the well-being of other people, not everybody operates this way. Some people are more concerned with facts and efficiency than they are feelings. So interrupting them really won't hurt them. They'll get over it quickly and move on.

Even though your gift is listening, you'd do well to practice interrupting when you're with extroverts. Treat it like you would learning another language. In this case, you're just learning another way to communicate. The more you practice jumping in, the more comfortable you'll feel when it's time to add your two cents.

When You Get Cut Off
The same logic applies to interruptions. If you've mustered up the energy - and courage - to interrupt and share your ideas, *expect* one of your extroverted colleagues to interject and cut you off. When this happens, be prepared to recapture the conversation. Finish your thought. At the end of the day, you'll be happier you shared what you wanted to share, and you'll spare yourself the seemingly never ending introspection that follows a bad meeting - the kind where you think back to what you wish you would have done and replay it over and over again in your head.

Don't Undervalue Your Insights
Another problem with the meetings, that drives most introverts batty, is the quality of the content being shared. Because introverts process internally, they usually reserve only gold nuggets for sharing with the outside world. Meaningless small talk and empty hot air drive them nuts. It's for this reason that many introverts undervalue what they have to add to a conversation. The last thing they want to do is add to the pile of meaningless fluff being tossed about a room. They want, rather, to share only deep insights and to make substantial contributions to the conversations. As a result of their high standard, a lot of their good ideas go unsaid.

To combat this phenomena, realize that a lot of what you may hesitate to share could actually help the extroverts in the room. Try to be easier on yourself and not hold yourself to such a high standard. Be a little freer with what you'd like to share. The thoughts you may consider air headed and unhelpful might actually benefit a lot the people in the room. They don't mind hearing unfinished thoughts.

Show Them Your Thought Process
Other challenges arise from the different ways introverts and extroverts process. A big one is that extroverts don't always understand how introverts come up with their ideas because introverts do a lot of thinking in their heads. There's no thought process trail for an extrovert follow. But introverts can overcome this challenge by doing a "think aloud."

Suppose, for instance, that that you're participating in a meeting for the purpose of helping a student make better behavioral choices. During your time with colleagues, you've been mulling over all the factors: the student's home life, his peer relationships, his past academic history, and his motivation - or lack of it - for learning. Suddenly, in your mind, you put the pieces together and come up with an innovative solution - one which you're excited to share with colleagues. So you do. The only problem is that they wonder how you came up with the idea and if it makes sense, considering all the factors. They want to see how you arrived at the solution.

This would be a great opportunity to incorporate a "think aloud" as you do for your students. Intentionally, take your colleagues on a journey through the thoughts and mental steps you took in your mind, and show them how you came up with the solution. By doing this, you will increase their understanding, allow them to ask clarifying questions, and increase their overall buy-in.

Spend Some Time with the Agenda

Because most introverts aren't fast on-their-feet thinkers, they need to prepare in advance. Preparation is an introvert gift, so use it to your advantage. Find the meeting agenda. (Politely request one if you're not given it.) Then, anticipate possible questions, and determine what you'll need to know to be ready for the meeting. Make this process a habit.

Furthermore, instead of trying to come up with answers on the fly, try writing yours out. Get all of your data together. Grab whatever student artifacts you'll need. Then, jot down some notes. You don't have to spend a lot of time. Just take five minutes and brain dump, or bullet point what you'd like to say. Remember, this process is just for you.

Keep in mind that, as an introvert, you're an excellent researcher and advance preparer, and you are also the kind of person who needs time to think things through. So be kind to yourself, and make time to do all of these things *before* the meeting. If you're worried this will take a while, put a time limit on your preparation. Cut it off after five to ten minutes. You'll be amazed by how that minuscule bit of preparation will transform a forty-five minute meeting.

Get to Know the Folks Involved

A lot of meeting conflict and animosity is the result of lack of trust and relationship. When we don't know other people, we have a hard time giving them the benefit of the doubt, and we have little relational capital to draw on. This makes meetings uncomfortable. We end up investing energy protecting ourselves and our reputations rather than accomplishing important objectives and tasks. But this doesn't have to be the case.

You can avoid a lot of bad feelings during meetings by spending a bit of time on a regular basis with the people in your building. Talk to your colleagues as you see them throughout the week. Ask them about their personal lives. Then, with what you learn, follow up, and ask specific questions about how things are going. Be considerate, and write them notes of appreciation and celebration when appropriate. You might consider sending small gifts or tokens of appreciation on birthdays or other holidays. In short, be a thoughtful coworker. This advance relational investment will completely change the climate of your meeting.

I know this advice seems contradictory to what I said earlier about moving with purpose. But it doesn't have to be. The reality of working with people is that you have to strike a balance between getting your work done and building positive relationships. So do make some time to talk with your colleagues. But I'd advise putting careful thought into the ways and times in which you do so.

Another strategy that you can apply to build positive relationships with your coworkers is to ask them for help. People like to be needed. I learned this lesson unexpectedly. For a grad class, I was writing a long paper and needed some statistics and background information on a grant our district had received. The only way to get the information I needed was to call our district language arts supervisor. At first, I was hesitant to contact her. I saw her as an in-charge, domineering personality. But when I went ahead and emailed her, she offered to talk with me on the phone. She sacrificed some of her personal time - over the summer, no less! - and gave me a generous amount of background information on the grant. She, then, offered to fill me in on whatever else I needed. My thoughts about her changed during that phone call, and my meetings with her have been different ever since. In fact, when colleagues complain that she's a little overbearing, I usually defend her, now that I've gotten to know her better.

Focus on Giving Credit

All people are hungry for affirmation and approval. We naturally seek it for ourselves. We don't, however, naturally give it to others. Whenever it's possible, strive to affirm and applaud people in the presence of others - particularly their supervisor. It's amazing the kind of positive impact these actions can have on your relationship.

At the beginning of this year, I was in a meeting with a colleague, going over some new teaching resources. Her supervisor was there, and the two of them were updating me on what I needed to be doing in my classroom. That's when I remembered some great new ideas my colleague had sent via an online learning system. I really liked the ideas she'd shared, so I told her and thanked her in front of her supervisor. And it just so happened that one of her goals was to share more resources via that technology, so her supervisor was impressed. My colleague was more than pleased to receive a compliment in front of her.

In several more recent meetings, I've been able to give credit to grade level colleagues for the above-and-beyond work they've been doing with students. One of them had created several effective behavior plans that had been helping students get their work done and stay on track. I gave her credit for her work and complimented her for her work in front of my colleagues. At the end of the day, after I'd forgotten about what I'd said, she came over to my room to thank me. She told me that the words meant a lot to her. A few well-spoken kind words can transform the atmosphere of any meeting.

Follow Up

Finally, as much as you'd like to share all of your best thoughts during meetings and no matter how much you prepare and politely interrupt so that you can do just that, there'll still be times when you have a brilliant brain child or a meaningful insight *after* the meeting ends. Don't beat yourself up for this. It's just how you work.

Expect this to happen, and resolve to employ one of your other introverted strengths - writing. If you don't get a chance to share a great idea or thought during the meeting, share it via email afterward. Email is your place to shine. While extroverts are better in the moment, introverts tend to present themselves more eloquently in writing. So take a little time to process and type out your thoughts. Mind you, try to keep your email to-the-point, and make it succinct because no one likes to read giant paragraphs. But remember: Late ideas can still be great ideas.

If you consistently and regularly employ these tactics, I'm confident that you and your coworkers will benefit and be happier with your contributions in the workplace.

PART THREE

Part III: Find Out What Energizes You

CHAPTER EIGHT

Your Unique Strengths

Introvert teachers, like all other people on our planet, possess unique strengths and gifts. They have the capacity to think and do what no extroverted teacher ever could. Unfortunately, the work of teaching is primarily an extroverted activity. Each school day calls introvert teachers to be "on" almost nonstop, and while introverts are capable of doing excellent work in the outer world, their best and greatest contributions will always flow out of the inner world of their minds. The question becomes, then, *How do introvert teachers integrate their natural gifts into their teaching?* With some creative thinking and intentional work, you can adapt the way you approach your work so that it better integrates your gifts and natural wiring. And in the following chapter, we'll discuss just how to do it. But for now, we need to start by determining what your unique strengths are. Fortunately, there are a variety of proven strategies to help you do just that.

Personality Tests

When it comes to figuring out what you love and are good at, personality tests can be a big help. There are a variety to choose from, each with its own strengths and weaknesses. The classic tried and true personality test is the Myers-Briggs. It's the most widely used and trusted. The Myers-Briggs classifies people into 16 personality types based on four pairs of type characteristics which include: introversion and extroversion, sensing and intuition, thinking and feeling, and judging and perceiving. After you take the Myers-Briggs Type Indicator (MBTI), you end up with a four-letter combination such as ISFJ that describes how you interact with the world, take in information, make decisions, and organize your life.

The MBTI will give you a unique and specific look into what energizes you, how your mind works, and what drains you. You'll discover why you think differently than other people, and you can use what you learn to restructure your life so that it's more productive and enjoyable. One particular benefit of the MBTI is that it identifies the primary (dominant function) and secondary (auxiliary function) strengths of each personality type. This information will help you quickly figure out what you *love* to do and where your gifts lie. You can also use this newfound knowledge to evaluate your current job and ask, "How frequently do I employ my greatest strength in my daily work?" There's a strong correlation between how much your job incorporates your strengths and your satisfaction with it.

Another great personality test is Strength Finders. This assessment describes you via your five greatest strengths. After you work through about 30 to 45 minutes of questions, you'll get a printout with descriptions of things you do well. As with the Myers-Briggs information, you can use your strengths to assess how well and frequently you use your greatest gifts on the job.

DISC is another common assessment tool. The assessment, however, differs from the MBTI in that it's a norm-based test: it aims to tell you how strong your personality traits are *compared with* a group of other people who possess similar traits. The MBTI only tells you if you're one personality or another. It doesn't measure the degree to which you possess a personality trait.

All three of these tests are helpful, and there are yet other tests. The more assessments you take, the better you'll understand yourself, and the more insight you'll have into how best to approach your work in a way that utilizes your core gifts.

As a caveat, I recommend taking the *paid* versions of these assessments. While you can find free versions online, they're knockoffs and aren't usually a product of research and careful study, so you may get what you pay for, and your results may be inaccurate. Keep in mind that you're aiming for insight - not misinformation.

Success Stories
Another great way to identify your strengths is to recall past successes. Think back to different stages of life, and list *your* success stories: The times when you did something you were incredibly proud of. Take a month and journal whatever comes to mind. Think about the whole of your life. Keep a pen and paper - or smart phone - with you. The ideas will come rolling in when you least expect them. Ask yourself, *What was I proud of when I was a kid? Where did I stand out as a teenager? In college? As an adult?* Write down all that you can think of, and piece together *your* story.

As a first or second grader, I wrote a poem about spring that was more like a fourth grader's work. I always enjoyed playing with words: Dad and I were constantly making up puns. In fifth grade, I'd make up jokes, and they always involved some kind of unique word play. It was also around this time that my teachers gave me positive feedback on my writing.

As I grew older, I could do other things most of my peers couldn't - such as make up lyrics to a song or wrap extemporaneously. And unlike most of my peers, speech class was my favorite in high school. Then, even in college, no matter what class I was in, I enjoyed writing papers most.

The crazy thing is that it took me years to realize what I was good at. I was generally a decent student. I studied hard, did my best, and enjoyed learning. The same may be true of you. Don't get frustrated if your greatest strength or talent isn't immediately obvious. Just try to come up with ten to fifteen vignettes.

Then, weave them together into a comprehensive story. In the *Feedback from Others* section, I'll show you how to solicit input from people who know you well to add even more to your story. Then, in the section entitled Reflection, I'll give you some suggestions on how to look for patterns and interpret your story.

Trial and Error

As you seek to determine what excites you and what you're best at, pay attention to your day. Start to be a first-class noticer in terms of what you enjoy and what you're good at. What parts of the day give you the most energy? Conversely, what parts of the day drain you? Consider keeping a journal where you can record your observations, and plan to do this for several weeks.

As you make the extra effort to attend to your strengths and interests, you'll be surprised by what you find. It's amazing how much extra information you can collect when your brain is focused on something new.

You may, however, find that nothing in particular about your work gets you fired up. If this describes you, it's time to try some new things. Some personalities grow the most when they explore and try what they've never tried before. There's no telling what you may find out about yourself when you start dabbling. My wife had a friend who only discovered she liked running in her fifties. But from that time on, she ran daily.

When you think about what to explore, think back to what got you excited as a kid and what other people said you were good at. I've only been writing regularly for about a year now. But I knew I always wanted to do it. I had an interest in it, and other people said I was pretty good at it. So I started writing, and I'm so glad that I did. What untapped potential and suppressed interests are hiding away in you?

Feedback from Others

Another great way to get feedback on what you're good at is to ask the people who know you best. I learned this strategy from Jonathan Milligan of BloggingYourPassion.com. Write down the names of five to ten people who know you well. Then, give each of them a call, send them an email, or shoot them a text. Ask, "What are my top two strengths? When you think of me, what do you think I'm good at?" Ask people that you know will want to help you. And don't feel bad about doing it! Usually, friends, family, and coworkers are more than happy to share an encouraging word.

When you get the results back, analyze the data. Do you see any patterns? Do others say your great at helping people resolve conflicts? Are you creative? Are you an incredible host? Pay attention to the details, but give extra attention to trends you notice.

Reflection

Eventually, you'll want to reflect on all that you've learned about yourself and try to synthesize the key takeaways. Again, look for patterns and trends. What stands out? What really rings true with you? Journal your thoughts, and add to them whenever you come away with a new insight. Bounce your thoughts off people who really know you well - but don't let them define you or box you in.

Take your time, and don't rush the process. Remember that the road to self-understanding is lifelong. "Aha" moments *will* come along the way. So keep learning, and stick with it. The rewards will be worth your effort.

Now that you're on a path to discovering - or confirming - your greatest strengths, we can explore how you can better integrate them into your current teaching position. That's the subject of the next chapter.

CHAPTER NINE

Working With Your Strengths

In this chapter, we'll get practical and tactical. On the following pages, you'll find several ideas on how you can integrate your strengths and introverted personality into what you do as a teacher. By no means is this an exhaustive list. The ideas here are meant to get you started and to catalyze your own creativity. The extent to which you integrate your gifts and passions into what you do is limited by your imagination only.

Less Is More

One of the most important principles to keep in mind is the principle of *less*. The best leaders in the world know that "Less is more." They know that focusing on a few things they excel at and delegating everything else gives them energy and benefits their organization. The same principal applies to you as a teacher. The more you can focus on what you do best, the better the quality of your work will be and the more excitement you'll have for your job.

Admittedly, this is also one of the challenges of teaching. Teachers, in many ways, are jacks of all trades. We're expected to instruct, police, coach, counsel, administrate, inspire, cast vision, and so on. So how can we cut back? How do we even focus on what we do best? Here are four suggestions.

1. Incorporate What Gives You Energy

A great starting place is to try to incorporate what gives you energy. If you know you love to work with technology - and you're good at it - create as many tech lessons as you can. Center your work around technology as much as you're able to. Become the tech guru for the building. If you're a musician, use your musical abilities to teach. Write and play songs to teach content. The same goes for anyone blessed with design skills. My sister has a knack for color, patterns, and fonts. Her room inspires her students. Work the way you love to work. Your passion will shine through, and it'll energize both you and the people around you.

2. Stop Comparing Yourself with Others

While you work, beware of comparing yourself with others. Those who compare never win. I know from experience. For a long time, I tried to be an extrovert. I tried to have a high-energy, conversation-driven classroom that some of my colleagues had. I also tried to be domineering and in charge. Neither of these teaching approaches is bad. They work if the right person is using them. But what I've found works for me is an organized, listening-driven classroom, with a touch of humor. It's my style. The only way you'll be happy and effective as a teacher is when you're being true to yourself.

3. Work with Coworkers

If you find that you're not the best planner or you want to spend less time on copies - or whatever you're trying to get away from - consider collaborating with a colleague. Hands down, this has been one of the best moves I've made. My neighbor and I plan together almost daily. The time we spend together has saved me days - maybe weeks - of planning.

Together, we're twice as productive. He's got a great handle on the curriculum, and I'm a bit more organized. So, when we team up, we create something more interesting and efficient. In addition, this year, my colleague has been making a lot of the copies for both us. In the time he's making copies, I file documents in Evernote for next year, and I also tag assessments with standards so that we can analyze data for report cards. Working together with a colleague frees your time. You spend far less time doing what you dislike and lots more doing what you enjoy.

4. Leverage Technology

Technology can be a curse or a blessing. Sometimes, it's a total waste of time. A few years ago when I should have been working on a literature review for a grad class, I bought a software program, Dragon Dictation, to speed up my word output. But I ended up having to learn and set up the program when I should have been writing. Bad move. Old fashioned typing would have done just fine. There was no need for me to change anything.

While change for the sake of change is wasteful, there is such a thing as good change. When it comes to technology, there are a lot of great changes you can make. The right technology will save you hours of monotonous grading and data tracking. It'll improve your relationships with parents. And it'll take your instruction to a whole new level. I'm a big fan of Screencast-o-matic, Evernote, Gradecam, and some other programs that you can learn more about in the Tech Tools chapter. For now, suffice it to say that if something is a real nuisance, there's probably a technology out there you can implement to save time, (and, if you're smart about it, you can get your District to pay for it.)

Strengths in Action

For the first time this year, I'm thinking of ways to incorporate my strengths into what I do. Let me give you a quick picture of what this looks like for me so that you'll have more ideas how you can make it work for you. My strengths are writing, interpersonal relationships, technology, and music.

I have my kids journal for the first five minutes of class each day. I also have them journal when they arrive at school and before they go home. In the morning, they write two things they're thankful for, two goals, and an affirmation for the day. Before they go home, they write two things that they achieved and one thing they learned. I enjoy teaching them the discipline of daily writing and showing them how they can improve over time.

I don't always do a great job of this, but I'm trying to incorporate basic social skills into every day as well. In the past I used to make my kids shake my hand when they first arrived, but with all the colds and viruses that go around each year, I don't do that anymore. Now, I just try to encourage them to say "Hello" while making eye contact. I enjoy helping the kids resolve conflict and reconcile.

Tech solutions give me energy too. As I mentioned above, I've found several computer applications that speed up grading and help with filing. A colleague and I have also made video updates this year to share with parents to let them know what's happening at school. I've made videos to capture the math skill of the day and to review the writing process so that students who want to review at home can go back and watch them later. If something takes a lot of energy and I feel it could be much more efficient, I love looking for a tech solution to the problem. My third grade colleagues know this, and they'll ask me from time to time for help when they encounter tech issues. I like being the guru for our hallway.

Last, I've experimented with writing songs to teach content. I play the guitar and enjoy writing lyrics. I've written grammar, reading, science, and writing songs to reinforce what we're learning in class. When I was first starting out, I wrote a rap to pump kids up for the state standardized assessment, and it played a large role in getting me the job that I have today.

I don't always get to use what I love. But the more I incorporate what makes me unique, the more I find I enjoy my job. As you incorporate more and more of your strengths, you'll find that you like your work more and more too.

In the next section, we'll investigate ways you can keep your focus and get more done in the same amount of time. In short, we'll help you tame your schedule.

PART FOUR

Part IV: Taming Your Schedule

CHAPTER TEN

Identifying Your Priorities

In earlier chapters, I pointed out that much of what bothers introverted teachers is noise: too much activity overstimulates an introvert's mind! But noise is more than just sonic stimulation. It extends to the busyness and diverse responsibilities that come with every teaching job.

In the first four or five years that I taught, I felt overwhelmed. I wrestled with what to do next. Should I grade, or should I plan? Should I work on an extracurricular assignment, or should address a behavior issue? A lot of the work I did was last-minute because I hadn't established priorities. I hadn't taken the time to decide what was really important. When I finally determined to put first things first, I stopped bringing home work on nights and weekends - at least most of the time, and, in general, I was far happier.

In order to enjoy your work, you need to cut through the craziness and determine where *your* priorities lie. You need to focus on the right tasks so that you can do great work and avoid burnout. Do yourself a favor you'll never regret, and figure out what really matters when it comes to your work. Here is how to get started.

Ask Your Supervisor

Unless you're the principal, you're responsible to a supervisor who, in turn, is responsible for your productivity. Don't waste anytime in seeking out what that person thinks your priorities should be. Ask her.

A friend of mine, who was not a teacher, always made sure he did this. When faced with a number of projects - too many to fit into the time he'd been given - he brought all of them to his supervisor and asked him to rank them in order of importance. That way, he never had to worry about what to do next. He knew his supervisor would be pleased with the preference he'd given each project.

I was hesitant to ask my principal at first. I didn't know any teachers that had talked with her, but I found out that she was more than happy to talk about priorities. She recognized my desire to steward my time wisely, be more productive, and more efficient, rather than thinking I was just trying to get out of work.

If you do have a principal who thinks that your choice to become a teacher means that you should be a slave to teaching at all hours, do your best to ignore him. Instead, make every effort to be exceedingly productive in the time that you do work at school, and demonstrate how you can get work done in the time given you. He will probably come to admire the wisdom of your way.

Mind the Pareto Principle

Not all work is equally meaningful and effective. Some of the things we do yield greater results. The Pareto Principle states that 20 percent of the work you do produces 80 percent of the results. Make your goal, then, to discern what that 20 percent is, and to focus your effort on that work. It will save you a ton of time in the long run and keep you from frittering away precious hours on stuff that really doesn't matter in the end.

Plan Until You're Blue in the Face

The one activity that, more than anything, has made a difference for me is planning. It's definitely in the 20 percent that produce 80 percent of the results. In fact, it's probably my number one priority.

I didn't used to think that way. I was hesitant to spend so much time planning because my educational training led me to believe my plans had to be formal, straight from the instructional design handbook. But that thinking led me astray. I've since learned that planning doesn't have to be a formal process. A lot of my best planning work is the thinking that I do in the car as I drive to school, as I walk to art or music to pick up my kids, or as I'm reflecting at the end of the day. It's the little ideas that pop into my head when I realize what my students are struggling with in the middle of the lesson - my reflections on formative assessments - that make the biggest difference.

Don't feel as though you have to plan on a certain document or in a certain way, but do plan - especially long-term! It will save you hours and hours of wasted time. In general, the more you plan - and the more long-range planning you do - the more successful you will be. You'll be able to be more creative as you integrate different subjects into cohesive projects. You'll experience less stress as you anticipate time crunches and windows of opportunity. And you'll have a better idea of how much time you can give to units when you know how much is available down the pike.

As I mentioned earlier, consider working with a coworker for lesson plans, especially if you're more of a fly-by-the-seat-of-your-pants kind of teacher. The accountability and idea melding that take place when you work with your colleague will do wonders for your classroom and, just as importantly, your time.

Remember Parkinson's Law

One of the biggest difference-making principles I've learned since I began teaching is Parkinson's Law. Parkinson's law states that tasks expand to fill the time allotted for their completion. In other words, the amount of time you set aside to complete your work is the amount of time your work is going to take. This can work for you or against you, depending on how you approach your work.

I used to let tasks - especially the ones I didn't like - steal my time. I built them up in my mind and anticipated them taking forever. This is what a lot of procrastinators do, according Neil Fiore, the author of The Now Habit. Fiore says previewing and thinking about a distasteful task is a lot like pressing your nose up against the base of a sky scraper and peering up to the top. Getting to the top - finishing the job - seems insurmountable.

Whether you're a procrastinator or not, you can get a lot more done by reducing the amount of time you set aside to finish tasks. When you're forced to work with less, you'll be apt to start more quickly. And starting is often the most difficult part for procrastinators. Cutting back on the available time will also force you to prioritize and keep you from wasting time on unimportant matters. If you do procrastinate, you'll get burned once and learn for next time.

If you're hesitant to try cutting back on the time you give yourself to get a task done and you don't think you can do it, just wait for when you're given more responsibility to show you Parkinson's Law in action. As we get older, each of us has more and more to do, like it or not. We learn to finish responsibilities that used to take us forever more quickly out of necessity. Take me, for example. I used to spend hours planning lessons my first few years. But now, with a family and other commitments, I make sure to knock out the majority of my plans during my forty-five minute planning block each day.

Do yourself a favor and experiment with this principle. The more you force yourself to do more with less, the more productive you'll become.

Decide Ahead of Time

It's easy to get sucked into a black hole of commitments in the school environment. As I mentioned before, everyone wants you to lead a club, coach a team, tutor, supervise, and volunteer in your "free time." But they also still expect you to get your teaching work done.

When I first started teaching, I coached volleyball and took graduate school classes at the same time. During that time, I committed to a small group at church. I'd bit off more than I could chew. I got sick a lot and spent most of the year running on fumes. I could have saved myself a lot of frustration and difficulty by deciding on my priorities ahead of time so that I could honor my introversion.

In the same way that long-term planning will save you time and effort in the classroom, it will also spare you in life and in the rest of your teaching responsibilities. Remember that, as an introvert, you have limited energy and you need to make time to recharge. It's unwise, therefore, to bite off more than you can chew and overcommit. Caring introvert teachers are especially prone to overcommit. Everybody needs you to volunteer and wants a piece of you. The volunteer recruiter has no idea what else is on your plate so he throws his best pitch at you and convinces you to sign up for one more thing. You dutifully agree because you *don't want to let him down*, only to go home and bang your head up against the wall. Don't do it anymore! Learn from your mistakes or the mistakes of others.

Before the start of the year - or sometime soon during this year - sit down with your calendar and think back to what involvement you really enjoyed. Was there a committee or team that meant a lot to you? Plan to do that. Also, consider how much time you'll need to recharge. How much downtime will you need on a weekly, monthly, and annual basis? Pencil it in on your calendar.

Steven Covey had a powerful illustration where he poured big rocks and little rocks into jar. The big rocks were important priorities - family, friends, vacation, and personal growth. The little rocks were time wasters - TV, interruptions, busywork, and the like. Covey had people put both size rocks into a jar as an illustration. The only way ALL the rocks would fit in, however, was when people started with the big rocks, the most important priorities. If people started with the little rocks, the unimportant time wasters, there would not be enough time for the big rocks, the truly important priorities. I commend this approach to you. Decide what matters to you, and make time for it. Then, you can tell people that you just don't have time to help when they ask - and you'll be speaking truthfully.

Master Your "No"

Another way you can protect yourself from overcommitment is to master a good "NO." *No* is wonderful word, and you should learn to love it. Don't worry. No doesn't have to hurt other people, and it doesn't always communicate that you don't care. Actually, no just gives people the facts that they need. If people take a no personally, that's a problem that they need to work through on their own.

Furthermore, there are ways to say "no" without offending someone. A good no can even strengthen your relationship with another person. So the next time you want to tell someone no but are having trouble spitting it out, try the following, which I learned from Michael Hyatt of MichaelHyatt.com.

First, start by thanking the person for asking you to help them. Next, affirm that you would really like to help but you are unable to commit at this time. Don't beat around the bush. Be honest, and tell the truth, and don't worry about cooking up excuses. Finally, if possible, connect the person with other resources, and offer to help at another time, if you'd really like to. Here's an example.

Colleague: "Hey, Bo. You're just the guy I wanted to see. I'm starting up an elementary volleyball league, and I remembered that you were a great volleyball player and also coached at the high school for several years. You'd have a lot of experience and knowledge to share with the guys. We'd love for you to be one of the coaches in our new league. I'm sure the players would love you, and we'd be so grateful. Would you consider helping us out?"

Me: "Thanks so much for asking. That was really thoughtful of you to think of me. I do enjoy volleyball, and the league you're putting together sounds awesome. At this time, however, I won't be able to help you out. Thanks again for asking. If you're interested in other coaches, I can try to connect you with a few friends who might be interested."

Finally, when in doubt, ask for time to think the decision over. You'll never regret asking for more time. With the extra time, think long and hard about what you're getting yourself into - the good, the bad, and the ugly. And then when you need to say it, say "NO!"

The more you integrate these principles, the more focused and productive you'll be. In addition, you'll lose less energy. So now that you've got some ideas for how you can preserve your energy, let's look into how you can recharge both at work and away from it.

PART FIVE

Part V: Re-energizing

CHAPTER ELEVEN

A Few Good Men

That introverts don't like or need people is nothing short of heresy. We do. It's just that we value depth and longevity in relationships, and we're more likely to have fewer friends. But those few friendships we do have mean a lot to us.

As an introvert teacher, don't underestimate the importance of a good confidant. You need people who will encourage you, cheer you on, mentor you, and work alongside you. These kinds of relationships will keep you going during the difficult days, weeks, and years. In this chapter, I'll explain *why* these relationships are important as well as how you can cultivate them.

Peer-to-Peer Collegial Relationships

I'm sure you know what it's like to have a trying day, the kind that leaves you spent and exhausted. You have to fight the kids from the first bell to the last, and your efforts seem to have made little impact. One of the best things you can do when you've had a tough day is to share your frustrations with a friend.

As an introvert, you need to get your thoughts out of your head. You need input and feedback, or else you're liable to beat yourself up for not making the progress you'd wished to make. A peer you can trust who's in the trenches with you will be able to lend a sympathetic ear and commiserate, and you'll be able to return the favor when she needs it.

Just be careful to keep your venting from turning into a complaining session. That won't benefit you or your colleague. Focus on the problem solving aspect, and then move on.

Solid peer relationships are an opportunity for you to spur others on and to be spurred on by others. You don't need a ton of these. One or two may suffice. But you want someone to whom you can turn when you're having a tough day who'll help you ground your thoughts and feelings in reality and keep your mind under control. Usually, the best partner is someone you work with closely and see on a regular basis, but this doesn't have to be the case. Think of someone with whom you could connect, and make a habit of "clearing the air" inside your head before you leave for home.

Mentors

In addition to a trustworthy peer, a mentor is a must-have, if you can find a worthy one. He doesn't have to be an all-knowing sage. Most mentors won't be able to teach you *everything* or meet all your needs, as Jeff Goins, author of *The Art of Work,*   points out. Just look for someone who can help you grow in an area in which you'd like to make some progress, or find someone who can help you develop your gifts.

During my first two years of teaching, I consistently met with another more experienced teacher. After our meetings, I almost always left encouraged. I never told that other teacher that he was a mentor to me, but I knew it all along. He helped me put my teaching into perspective and taught me that you've got to try and fail sometimes to get better. In his words, "There's only one way to get experience."

He also helped me understand that every teacher has different gifts and that you've got to be yourself. Trying to do what someone else does will never pay off because you're not him. I learned from his interactions with kids, and I learned from the way I saw him work with his colleagues. His diligence with grading, in order to give his students feedback, is something I still think about to this day, and I loved his attitude of constant learning and growth.

I learned just what I needed to learn from our informal conversations and short times together. Keep in mind that mentoring doesn't have to be *formal* to make your life better.

Friends

This goes without saying, but I'll say it anyway. You've got to have some great friends too.

After a long, hard weak, it's tempting to curl up into a ball inside your house, and hide away with a book or your computer until the start of the next week. It's not always wrong to do this; sometimes you just need to recharge. But one of the best things you can do for yourself is to spend some time with great friends.

It's my friends and my wife who remind me that there's way more to life than my teaching job. For this reason, I need to regularly invest in and spend time with friends. I need to forget about whatever job-related concerns are bothering me and tune in to their needs. Turning my energies from my own worries and thinking about others puts me in a more productive state of mind. It keeps me from worrying, affords me the pleasure of meaningful relationships, and adds another facet of purpose to my life. My friends help me relax and unwind.

More extroverted friends will help you get out of the house. If you're like me, you'll resist it, but we all need it from time to time.

The time you spend with friends doesn't always have to be away from home. Some of the best memories I have are hanging out with friends at my house. We played board games, watched movies, shared a meal, and enjoyed each other's company around a bonfire.

I was also lucky enough to have the kind of friends who came into my classroom to help me set up for the year. They helped me prepare bulletin boards, arrange desks, and clean up my classroom. Without their help I know wouldn't have been ready for the first day of school.

Great friends will encourage you and give you perspective. They'll help you grow to be a better person and, therefore, a better teacher.

In the next chapter, we'll look at how side projects can give you a creative outlet and increase your effectiveness as an educator.

CHAPTER TWELVE

The Role of Side Projects

As much as you might like your job, teaching won't meet all of your needs. There are some things that you enjoy doing that you won't get to do in your classroom. If the extroverted school culture doesn't cater to all of your introvert needs, no problem. With a little forethought, you can make time for your other passions and gifts. This work you do outside of teaching will fuel you in the classroom.

In this chapter, I'll share a few specific reasons why investing in your passions is a good idea as well as some ways you can make time for them.

Why You Need Side Projects

As an introvert, you're wired for projects, and, depending on your personality, you will enjoy them for various reasons.

If you're the organized type, getting things done energizes you. In the school environment, however, you don't have full control over what gets accomplished. You can encourage, inspire, and cajole your students, but at the end of the day, they are ultimately in control of the work they do.

This isn't the case when you're working on your own project at home. Many teachers love to garden because they can get dirty nurturing a seed to maturity. From the tiniest seed, a beautiful or delicious plant grows. Others like to sew or quilt. Again, you're in charge here. You determine the progress you make. You might even like doing chores. I've always somewhat enjoyed mowing the lawn. It gives me the chance to be outside and ponder, but best of all I get to see a pristine lawn when I finish. You don't always get to enjoy the final product when you teach.

Maybe you're more the creative type. If you like writing, recording music, drawing, painting, or shooting movies, your downtime is a chance to make something amazing. Just put in the time, and you'll be able to enjoy the product.

If you're not driven to get things done, you'll probably still enjoy projects. They give you a chance to go with the flow or lose yourself in something you love. For once you won't have to worry about the clock, your endless list of to-dos, or a stack of papers that needs grading. You can concern yourself with making that creation of yours, whatever it may be.

Although projects and works of any kind don't define you, they are a nice reminder that you are more than a teacher. When you do them, you can stop and remember, "I have other gifts to enjoy." Outside work and interests are a great way to develop relationships away from your workplace. My brother-in-law loves Mac computers. He and his dad have long been part of a Mac lovers group. It's a great way for him to meet people who share his passion for technology. If you're a seamstress, check out sewing blogs and online communities. Like to write? Find a writers guild. Hook up with people that like to do what you enjoy, and add to your life outside the classroom walls.

Projects also fuel your creativity within the classroom. It's been said that creativity is really just thinking outside the box. It's an ability to make connections that no one else has thought of yet. Some of the most creative people take ideas from unrelated disciplines and blend them together to create what's never existed before. Creativity is like a muscle: The more you exercise it outside the classroom, the stronger it will be when you need it inside school walls.

When I first got started in the classroom, I developed a tech obsession. What started as an attempt to build a classroom website exploded into several hours a night each weekend messing with and building wikis and Google Sites. More recently, I fed my passion for guitar, started a blog, and learned to podcast. All these interests come back around to inspire what I do in my classroom. Your best teaching ideas will often flow out of who you are and what you do. For this reason, you're stunting your growth as a teacher if you're not getting out and trying new things, dabbling in new opportunities, and enjoying side projects.

Making Time for Projects

With all of the teaching responsibilities on your plate, you may wonder how you'd ever have time for side projects. The truth is that you have time for that which you make time. And the number of ways that you can come up with extra hours for your other interests is limited only by your imagination. Personally, I've tried several strategies with varying success. What works for you will depend largely on your stage of life and personal preferences.

For a while I've stuck with a morning routine. I try to get to bed earlier, usually around 8 or 9 p.m. Then I wake up between 4 and 5 a.m. This way I get a solid 8 hours of sleep, but I'm still able to be up before most of my neighbors and family have stirred. Following this schedule I consistently have an hour to an hour and a half of time I can invest in projects first thing. I enjoy starting the day this way because it enables me to accomplish something significant before I ever arrive at school. In turn, that feeling of accomplishment gets my day started off on the right foot. And even if the rest of the day falls apart, I know my efforts during all of my waking hours weren't completely fruitless.

This schedule is beneficial if you're a morning person. It's also great when you have small children. You don't have to worry about interruptions, email, or phone calls. You have pure focus if you want it, something most introverts truly enjoy.

If getting up so early in the morning sounds crazy, you can also try fitting in your project time late at night at the end of the day. If you're more of a night owl, this schedule might fit you better. Then, once again, regardless of how your day went, you can finish on a positive note, making some progress in an area that's important to you. Bear in mind, however, that if you choose to work at night, you'll probably not have the same level of energy that you'd have if you woke up early, considering you'll have spent much of it during your work hours.

Finally, you may find that you're best able to make time for project work in between other responsibilities. Lately, I've getting a lot done in the time between my after school physical workout and when my wife gets home. Sometimes, as little as fifteen to thirty minutes before dinner is enough time to crank out 500 words on a book or a blog post. When it comes down to it, if you have the desire, the positive attitude, and commitment to consistency, there's no limit to what you can accomplish on a side project.

Sacrifices

And as with most things, you can't add more to your plate without giving something up. But take heart, the work you do on your projects that interest you is a happy exchange for less important things. For me, I've had to give up time watching TV and YouTube. I also don't play basketball in the mornings with colleagues anymore. I spend less time texting and surfing the web, but, as I alluded to before, I still have plenty of time for exercise, and I don't miss the time watching TV. From time to time, I'll fret about not catching the news, but I pick up what's going on in small talk, from scanning headlines each morning, and from family.

Side projects can be truly refreshing, but they won't meet all your needs. You need a regular diet of inspiration and ideas to stay positive and fresh. You need to invest in your personal growth, which is the final chapter in this section of the book.

CHAPTER THIRTEEN

Never Stop Growing

One of the best ways to build your resiliency and maintain a positive mindset in the midst of a demanding environment is to invest in your personal growth. Through regular, consistent investments of time, you can fuel your mind, revive your passion, and increase your resiliency. What's more, you'll improve your self-understanding and strengthen your skills, abilities, and passions.

The Role of Personal Growth

Cobie Langerak said, "If you are unwilling to learn (and grow) no one can help you. If you are determined to learn (and grow) no one can stop you." If you want to succeed as an introvert teacher and do your best work, you need to invest in personal growth. The work you put into developing your skills and abilities will yield greater results in the classroom. It will also open doors of opportunity and future options for you.

If, for instance, you'd like to invest in other teachers in the future, you need to have something to invest. But don't just count on the experience you'll gain over the years. Experience isn't always a good teacher. I recently read a story in a Steve Moore book about a boy who stuck a screwdriver in an electrical outlet. His father saw him from across the room just in time to recognize what was happening but too late to do anything about it. As the child inserted the screwdriver's metal shaft into a receptacle, he received a tremendous shock. Fortunately, the screwdriver's handle was rubber, so he wasn't hurt, just frightened. Like any good father would, the boy's dad ran over, picked him, and comforted him. When the boy finished crying, he said something his father never anticipated: "It did the same thing too me yesterday!" Apparently, he hadn't learned from his experience. Anybody can do the same thing for 20 years, but the best teachers are committed to a regimen of personal growth that helps them reflect on, critique, and modify their practice.

Effective teachers are resourceful as well, largely because of their personal growth plans. Leadership expert John C. Maxwell has spent years filing quotes, statistics, and stories from books he's read. As a result, he's got a wealth of information for the speeches he gives and the books he writes. He used to worry that he wasn't creative enough. Then he realized that he could use the creative ideas of others. Now he's one of the most creative people around. A commitment to personal growth will put the right ideas at your disposal when you or your team need them.

Finally, a personal growth plan will save you pain. People have spent their whole lives researching topics, and they've recorded their work in books. None of us needs to suffer needlessly. If we'd commit ourselves to learning from the successes and failures of other people, we could avoid a lot of trouble. I know I wished I'd have started investing in personal growth long before I actually did. It's hard to imagine how much pain I could have avoided with what I know now about planning, organization, priorities, and time management.

If you want to reach your potential and be the best teacher that you can be, and if you want to figure out how to best tailor your work environment to your individual strengths and needs, you need to invest in your personal growth. Committing to a personal growth plan makes you a model for students: they get to see a lifelong learner in the flesh.

Listen to Positive Audio

One of the best ways to invest in your growth is to listen to positive audio. By this, I mean audiobooks. You have a surprising amount of untapped time available to you throughout the day. Whenever you drive, do the dishes, or complete any other mindless chore, you have time that you could spend learning. Zig Ziglar says people who listen to positive and uplifting material, the kind that inspires and teaches you, on a regular basis are far more resilient than those who don't. The cells in their body store positive chemicals that help them bounce back whenever they experience setbacks and discouragement.

A great place to start, Ziglar explains, is to enroll in "automobile university." Devote your drive time to listening and learning, and play inspirational and informative books and podcasts whenever you get in the car. I find that when I do this on the way to work, I arrive with a better attitude and, consequently, have a better day. Similarly, when I listen to uplifting content on the way home after a bad day, I get home in a better mood and am better prepared to spend time with my family. If listening to music while you're in the car is important, consider committing either the ride to or the ride from work to listening to audiobooks. Then, leave the other part for music. Any investment you make in your personal growth will pay you back over time as you become a better thinker, problem solver, and generally a more positive person.

Read Every Day

You've probably heard it said that "Readers are leaders." It's true, considering most Americans read no more than part of a book each year. The people who commit to learning are the ones who wield the most influence.

Personal development guru Jim Rohn urged his audiences to read. He knew that reading can change your life because it gives you ideas, ideas that can improve your current situation, help you plan a better future, and help you serve the people around you. Rohn challenged people to think of reading as more important than food: While skipping a meal is okay, failing to read is not.

If you can read an hour each day, your life will change. But don't fret if you can't start there. Do what you can. Maybe fifteen or twenty minutes is where you need to begin. If you don't know where you'll find the time, try your lunch break, getting up a little bit earlier, or staying up a tad later.

This past year, I read more books than I've ever read in one year. The way I think about life changed. I gained tools that helped me plan, overcome procrastination, get more organized, make the most of a great idea, solve problems, communicate more effectively, and inspire people. In small ways, it changed my life. I can't wait to see what will happen as I continue reading.

Find Mentors

Your personal growth plan will be incomplete without mentors. I already addressed the benefit of learning from people older than you in an earlier chapter, but in this chapter, I will introduce the idea of peer mentoring.

One of the best ways to learn is to get together on a weekly, biweekly, or monthly basis with people who are in the same stage of life as you. When you get together with peers, you can swap the titles of books you're reading, share resources, and hold one another accountable for reaching personal growth goals. I'm currently in a peer group with two other guys. Once a month, we meet at Starbucks before work. I almost never leave our meetings without one great new idea. And I'm regularly encouraged to jump back into my goals with greater fervor. As running with a partner challenges you to keep moving and push yourself, meeting with a group will challenge you to strive to reach your potential.

Now that we've discussed the importance of personal growth and several ways you can re-energize, it's time to investigate how you can guard your time!

PART SIX

Part VI: Guarding Your Mental Energy

CHAPTER FOURTEEN

Getting Organized

Like it or not, the demand of each day's to-dos is an ever-present pull on your energy. Those writing papers you're trying to remember to grade, the parent you've got to respond to before tomorrow, and the children who need to make up their homework are stealing focus and energy from your mental reserve. Not to mention that the constant stream of paper coming across your desk is relentlessly building toward Mount Everest-like heights. If you don't have an organizational system that's helping you quickly and automatically prioritize, remember, file, delegate, and complete whatever projects are entering your physical and digital inbox, you'll be swamped and overwhelmed in no time.

Depending on your personality, you may or may not tend toward organization. But no matter who you are, two things are true: 1) you need a system of organization, and 2) your system can get better.

In this chapter, I'll share a few of the life-changing tips I learned from David Allen's book, *Getting Things Done*. For more detailed instructions on how to develop a powerful organizational system, check out his book!

Your Inbox
The first step to getting paperwork, tasks, and projects under control is to set up inboxes. You should have no more than two. One is digital and for email. The other is a physical inbox, such as a tray on your desk.

Don't allow yourself to create additional piles. Stick to two inboxes. If you have more than these two inboxes, you'll start to lose and misplace items, and this will stress you out. When your mind knows that you've only got two places to look, just two places through which all your projects and to-dos flow, you'll start to relax, but you've got to stick with this system.

Processing Your Inbox
Once you relegate your workflow to two inboxes, you'll be ready to start processing your work. Understand that for any work that comes across your desk, the ways you handle it are limited: you can only discard it, file it, delegate it, schedule it, or do it.

We run into trouble when we take too long to decide which of these things to do. You need a two-minute rule to prevent bottlenecks from forming according to David Allen. **No item that moves through your inboxes should ever take more than two minutes to process.** If it does, you'll just move the paper to another pile or folder, and you won't make any progress.

3 Key Tools

To discard, file, delegate, schedule, and do the work in your inboxes, you'll need a few key tools: 1) a to-do list, 2) a calendar, and 3) a filing cabinet. There are physical and digital versions of all these tools, and both work. I prefer the digital variety because they allow me to access my materials almost anywhere. But do whatever you're most comfortable with. In the next sections, I'll explain where each of these tools comes into play.

Throw It Out

Whenever you're processing an item in your inbox, first ask if you can throw it out. A lot of what you think is important isn't. Don't even open mass email or junk mail. Delete it. If there's a professional development opportunity you *know* you won't attend, throw that paper out. Don't allow useless information to pile up.

File It

There are, however, many documents you may want to refer to later. You need to put these in a place where you can quickly access them in the future. Most of the time, that place is a filing cabinet - either a physical or digital one. In today's age, I would recommend digitally filing as much of your paperwork and as many of your documents as possible. Optical Character Recognition (OCR) and keyword searches have made finding documents fast and easy, and you can take all of your documents with you thanks to smart phones.

I started using Evernote to file almost all of my school materials this year. (I'll tell you more about my system and the benefits of using it in the next chapter.) For now, just know that Evernote can save you a TON of time, and it's definitely worth looking into if you're looking for speed, organization, flexible filing, and efficiency.

While digital filing is handy, you can accomplish the same objectives with a physical filing cabinet too. And sometimes filing documents physically is faster. Whenever you physically file documents, a few principles will make you a more productive and effective filer. First, always keep extra hanging file folders and manilla file folders within arms reach. If you don't keep them within arms reach, you'll put off adding the folders, and your piles will grow. Second, keep your filing cabinet within arms reach. If you don't, you won't use it or you'll use it infrequently.

I used to keep my filing cabinet on the other side of the room, but that was a colossal mistake because I never used it. All it did was collect dust and take up space. I've since moved the cabinet beside my desk. Now, while I'm sitting at my desk, I can just pivot and drop whatever documents I want to file in the appropriate spot. It takes only seconds. I recommend that you do the same because this small change will change your organizational life.

Delegate It

There are tasks that you were never meant to do. For instance, sometimes your colleagues should be the ones who should respond to a parent's questions. Don't waste your time addressing questions the principal, school psychologist, counselor, or special area teacher are better equipped to answer. Forward inquiries and requests for help to the appropriate people ASAP.

Schedule It

You'll also run across tasks you need to accomplish that you can't do today. When you learn of an upcoming event or task that's not due the day you learn about it, don't leave it in your inbox. It'll mess with your psyche and steal your energy. Instead, determine whether or not to put the task on your calendar or on a to-do list. If the event is a meeting and it's time sensitive, get it on your calendar, and make sure to include any pertinent information you might forget in the notes of your calendar. If you run across a task that can be finished anytime before a certain day, put it on a to-do list.

Be careful to maintain only one to-do list. You don't want two or three of them in different spots. Your mind will only relax when you're recording tasks on a list that you check consistently. So plan to go back to the same list on a daily basis throughout the workweek.

A digital to-do list is beneficial because you can drag and drop tasks to reprioritize your work. As you work through your inbox, an item that was at the top of your to-do list earlier in the week might not look so important in the face of a new project. I like using Wunderlist for this reason. And it's free. Wunderlist also allows me to create subtasks for each of the tasks I create.

Finally, as you add tasks to your to-do list, make sure to note the date that they're due. If you're using a digital application, you can do this within the program. You might also want to consider marking the dates big projects are due on your calendar as well.

Do It

As you work through your inbox, make a goal to touch each of the items only one time. This applies to your physical and digital inboxes. Resist the temptation to look at something and then return it to the same pile for later. Remember: there are only so many things you can do with any one item in your inbox. Figure out what action to take. Then execute. The better you've set up each of the components of this system, the more quickly you'll be able to knock out your work.

To wrap this section up, I recommend creating a prioritized list of to-dos each day you come to work. When you arrive, take a look at your calendar and to-do list. Then determine what's important and urgent that you've got to get done for the day. Put that on your list. But also consider what's important that you'd like to make progress on. Add those items to your list too. Finally, prioritize, starting with time-sensitive meetings. Do your best to move the most important tasks to the start of the day. That way you'll be able to devote your best energy to the important things, and you'll be more likely to get those done.

Prioritize and work through your tasks and events on a daily basis, but also think long-term. Ask, *What do I need to get done this week?* And, *What needs to be completed in the next month, half a year, or year?* The further you can plan ahead and put first things first, the happier you'll be in the long run.

When you've got an organizational system, you'll starting knocking out the tasks you've been putting off. It's a great feeling. Now let's check out a few technology tools that'll make your work easier and more efficient.

CHAPTER FIFTEEN

Tech Tools

In your struggle to combat busyness and save time and energy, tech tools can make all the difference. There are a few that have really helped me over the past few years, and I've included them in the list below. Use this list however you wish. Take what you want, and leave the rest behind.

Gradecam

This tool saves me hours when it comes to grading. Gradecam is an automatic grading tool that uses your computer's webcam to scan printable bubble sheets. Turn any multiple choice or rubric-based assessments into a scannable test. Just create a printable scantron sheet, and print it off for each of your students. Then, the kids will fill in an ID number (I use the one our school assigns them, which they've already memorized.) and the appropriate answers, and you'll score their tests as soon as they finish by simply holding their paper up to your computer's camera. They get immediate results, and you save hours grading.

You'll also get an item analysis for each of the tests you create and scan. And you can compare students' performance on assessments over time. The paid version also gives you the ability to tag questions with standards so that you can determine what questions are giving your class the most trouble and double down on instruction where needed. One of my favorite parts of the Gradecam software is that you can automatically transfer your students' scores from Gradecam into your digital grade book when you finish collecting the test results. It's fast and easy.

Evernote

As I mentioned before, Evernote is my digital brain and the new filing system I use for almost all my documents. I collect lesson plans and materials, anecdotal notes, emails, resources I find on the web, parent notes, videos, and all kinds of other information. Evernote has powerful search features that enable you to search notes as well as documents in notes, for specific keywords. Its OCR capabilities even allow you to search pictures for keywords.

Now, whenever I get a paper in my school mailbox or at a faculty meeting, I pull out my smart phone, take a snapshot of the document as soon as I get it, save it to Evernote, tag it with appropriate labels, and then throw the sheet out on the spot. No more leaving meetings with a handful of documents to file. I do that right where I am and pitch the paper. It's cathartic.

Evernote has some wonderful collaborative features as well. Got a note you want to share? Just send the parent or colleague a private or public link. This year I used Evernote to put together an overview of each of my students' performance for fall conferences. I dragged a PDF of their report card into a note, added some comments, and inserted links to other notes with behavioral records. I even entered a snapshot of a pie chart from Class Dojo, a digital behavior tracking system which I'll explain in a minute. The whole process only took me about five minutes per student. There's really no end to what you can do with this tool.

In my mind, the best part of Evernote is its flexibility. Instead of putting a paper in a manilla folder in a filing drawer in my filing cabinet, I can apply as many labels as I want to the paper. So, when I get a newsletter from my principal for instance, I tag it with her name, the month, the year, the word "newsletter", and anything else I might remember. Then, later, when I need to dig it up, I can search for any one or combination of those tags. If for some reason that doesn't work, I can search for a keyword that was in the note. Evernote allows me to access a virtually endless amount of information in little to no time.

Google Drive

Drive is Microsoft Office for free with some extra features. Anyone who has a Google account has access to Drive, and anyone can get a free account. Google Drive has Word, Excel, and PowerPoint equivalents, and all of the programs allow you to collaborate with other people in real time online. Drive also has some excellent sharing features. Because you probably already know a lot about this program, I'll focus on two parts of Drive that I use all the time.

One of the programs is Sheets, Google Drive's Excel. I use Sheets on a daily basis for planning. My colleague and I organize all of our ideas and plans on a shared sheet. We designate a tab for each of the units we teach, and we break each unit into days using columns. This allows us to have a year's worth of plans in one spreadsheet. I love using Google Sheets because we can both access our plans anywhere we have internet; we don't have to be at school. We never have to worry about emailing each other our plans. We just need to save the link. As a matter of fact, I've bookmarked the link in the bookmarks bar of my Chrome browser because I access it so frequently.

The second part of Drive that I've used a lot in the past is Google Forms. When I'm looking to collect anecdotal records, I usually enter them into a form. A form is a digital survey with short-answer, text, multiple choice, and true or false fields. Once you create one, you can share it with others, use it as an assessment, or use it to collect and organize your own data. Any information you enter into a form automatically populates to a connected spreadsheet. You can designate a particular spreadsheet, or the form will create one for you. I've used forms to collect behavioral notes, track missed homework, and monitor the accommodations and modifications I've used with students. Forms are particularly helpful if you team teach because you and your coworker can enter and access data at any time, even simultaneously. If you opt to create a form to use as an assessment, Google has a Drive add-on called Flubaroo that you can set up to automatically grade student responses.

Symbaloo

More and more teacher-friendly digital resources are available online. That means there are a lot of websites to keep track of. You can go the traditional route of saving bookmarks in folders or a Diigo-like tool, or you can look into Symbaloo.

Symbaloo is a visual bookmarking tool that helps you organize and remember the websites you frequent as a teacher. I love how the site allows me to create a vignette complete with a logo and label for each of the websites I use. Each thumbnail image is hyperlinked: when I click it, it takes me to the webpage. And the vignettes appear beside each other in rows of tiles, organized by folders. If you haven't tried it, you need to. It makes bookmarking easy and convenient.

PassPack

Another challenge that comes with using a boatload of online tools is password management. You've probably got a 100 different passwords you need to manage. While you could write them on a piece of paper or keep them in a Word file, there's two problems in taking either of those approaches. First, they're insecure: anyone could steal your passwords. Second, you can't always take the information with you unless you want to carry a piece of paper in your wallet or purse all the time. That's where PassPack comes in.

The site stores all of your passwords in one place. It also gives you a place to record notes about each of your online accounts and links to the specific sites you regularly visit. The best part about PassPack is how secure it is. The site uses bank-level security encryption with three stages of security. It's safe enough that you could store your banking information on it.

LastPass

LastPass is another great password site. I'm using this one more and more for an important reason. When I visit sites, LastPass autofills my username and password, saving me boatloads of time and sparing me unnecessary frustration.

Suppose I want to log into Google, for example. I just navigate to the log in page. When I arrive, LastPass will recognize the page, and automatically insert my username and password. I don't have to worry about copying and pasting or remembering a random password. All I have to do is press *Log In*. I love it.

Class Dojo

Class Dojo is an all-in-one behavior management, parent communication, and data tracking application. It was created by teachers for teachers, and it's free.

With Class Dojo you import your students' names, and it sets up an avatar for each of them. Next, you create positive behaviors you want to reward and negative ones you want to discourage. A positive behavior I encourage is "respect", and the negative counterpart I discourage is "disrespect". Whenever a student is making respectful or disrespectful choices, I tell him to add or take away a point. He does this by clicking on his avatar and then clicking again on the appropriate behavior. At the end of the day, he'll have a cumulative number of points based on his behavior.

Dojo saves this data and graphs it for you, and you can view it over various date ranges, which is perfect for data meetings and parent-teacher conferences. In addition, parents can view their children's points in real time. So many of them naturally ask their kids what they were doing when they lost a point. If their child doesn't give them the full story, they can get the facts from you. Dojo also has a built-in messaging app where you can message individual parents, and they can message you back.

If you ever need to make whole-class announcements or want to share pictures and videos from school, Class Dojo's got you covered. It has a feature called Class Story that you can use to send images, video, documents, text, and links. Send homework reminders, school announcements, and surveys until your heart's content.

Screen-cast-o-matic
If you'd like to make screen recordings (videos of your computer screen) for students, parents, teachers, or anyone throughout the school day, this is a great tool to use. Screen-cast-o-matic allows you to record just your screen, your face, or your screen and face. You can use it for free, and you'll have access to a decent amount of features. But for just $15, you'll get a bunch of great editing tools that'll make recording videos super fun and easy.

I use Screen-cast-o-matic mainly for teaching and communication. If I'm showing kids how to structure an informational writing, for example, I may record myself walking through the steps on my computer. Then, after class, I post a link to Class Dojo so students can review the steps at home. Or if a student is out and misses the lesson, she can watch whenever she has time on a laptop in the classroom. Sometimes students need to hear the lesson another time. Once the lesson is recorded, the kids can listen to it as much as they need to.

This year, my colleague and I are using Screen-cast-o-matic to send out a monthly update. We make a short presentation on Google Drive, and we take turns narrating the slides and images and letting parents know what their kids have been up to as well as what's coming down the pike.

Wunderlist
In the last section I referred to my favorite digital to-do list: Wunderlist. Wunderlist is great because you can have it on multiple computers and devices.

Furthermore, you can create as many to-do lists as you want and house them all in the same place. Wunderlist enables you to add items, prioritize with drag and drop capabilities, and check off completed tasks. If you're collaborating with other people, you can even share a to-do list, which may save you more than a few emails.

Within each to-do, there's a place where you can set due dates and reminders, add notes and links, and even add subtasks. I love the subtask feature. It helps me a ton with report cards. I created a report card task. Then, within it, I created subtasks for reading, writing, science, and so on within that task. As I checked off each subtask, a progress bar on my report card task inched from the left to the right of my screen, letting me know how far I'd come and how far I had left to go.

The Wunderlist version I use is completely free and automatically synchronizes across your devices when you're in range of wifi or you're connected to a wireless network. I highly recommend it.

PART SEVEN

Conclusion

CHAPTER SIXTEEN

You Are Needed

As an introvert, it's too easy to compare yourself with other teachers in the extroverted world of teaching. So many of our colleagues are outgoing and get energy from their interactions with people. Just the other day after a morning professional development session, I spent my lunch reading alone in the cafeteria. I was really enjoying the quiet when I colleague from another school in the district spotted me as he was walking by. "Are you okay?" he asked. He was concerned that I was sitting alone reading a book, as if there were something wrong with me. "No," I told him. "This is actually fun for me." An expression of shock washed across his face.

Though people may not understand you or your need for silence and though you may feel as if you're swimming against the current, remember that you are valuable. There are many introverted students in the school where you teach who will benefit from your quiet gifts. They need to see a role model and to participate in a class where they're not expected to talk and interact frenetically. You're classroom may just be the one place where they can relax, be themselves, feel understood, and know that there's nothing wrong with them.

As you work, remember to take care of your needs. It's okay that you recharge and function differently than your extroverted colleagues. Take time to recuperate and do what you enjoy. Build in downtime during your day.

Remember also that one of the best ways to manage your energy is to find out what energizes you. Ask yourself, "What gets me excited?" Take personality tests. Seek the advice of people who know you well. Experiment. Then incorporate what makes you unique into the fabric of what you do at school. You and your students will love it.

As you work, set up boundaries with students, parents, and coworkers as appropriate. Don't be afraid to say no. Rather, find out what you *want* to say yes to, and be proactive. And even though this is going to take some effort, make sure that you invest in relationships. Find mentors. Build relationships with your coworkers. Pour into others who are coming up behind you. You won't regret it.

The world needs you, and the world needs to know what wonderful and unique introverted gifts you have to offer. Let your gifts shine.

CHAPTER SEVENTEEN

Thank You!

Thank YOU so much for taking the time to read this book. I hope it served you well! If it did, please share it with a friend or colleague. I'd love to hear your thoughts. You can connect with me on Facebook and Twitter or email me at bo_miller@ispeakpeople.com.

-Bo Miller

Made in the USA
Coppell, TX
17 September 2021